PERFECT BINDING

PERFECT BINDING

edited by

Alison and Malcolm Chisholm

First published in 2021
by Caleta Publishing

Copyright © contributors 2021

ISBN: 978-1-312-94651-4

Printed and bound by Lulu.com

FOREWORD

At this moment, the world is in the grip of a pandemic that has left families bereft and grieving, curtailed or skewed normal activities, and diminished all of our lives. Any and every glimmer of light in these dark days is to be welcomed and relished.

We hoped to celebrate our golden wedding anniversary on 10th July, 2021 with a party ... a holiday ... a crowd of friends and relations. We all know about the best laid plans. Instead, we looked back over fifty years of marriage and realised that our lives together have been bound by and blessed with poetry.

Poetry can entertain, inform, console, rage, sulk, fascinate, amuse, surprise, inspire, relax, befriend, heal, and engender hope. Poets are lovely, generous people, unfailingly willing to share their gifts. So this is our celebration. We decided to put together a collection of poems by 68 writers (we met in '68) whose lives have touched ours, whether by an occasional glance or inextricably interwoven.

The poems have not been arranged into neat themes, though there are some occasional points of contact. Instead, this is a book full of the joys of randomness. Be challenged, be surprised, be excited each time you turn the page.

We want to thank everyone who has kindly contributed to *Perfect Binding*, and hope that all who read it will gain as much pleasure from studying the poems as we did from compiling the anthology.

Alison and Malcolm Chisholm

For all those family and friends
who have touched our lives
in the past fifty years.

CONTENTS

Perfect Binding

**The poet addresses an occasional lover after
pushing twin beds together in a hotel room.**

Dearest, since we can do no other,
here on the bed that fate decrees
let us lie side by side together,
heads and shoulders, hips and knees
aligned along a central fissure
like pages in a paperback;
conjoined by heat and sticky pressure,
divided by a constant crack.

And thus, though circumstance divide,
we lie together, if bereft,
like vellum swelling either side
of this, our necessary cleft.
So let us live, and let us love,
proximity is written in
although we may not always have
the bliss of lying skin to skin.

So let us love, and let us live
as we are simply bound to do;
our numbers are consecutive,
our sense and syntax follow through.
If anyone should ever look,
we two will be forever found,
pages in one another's book;
not stitched, my love, but perfect bound.

Ann Drysdale

In Celebration

Let not the marriage of two trams admit derailment.
No – not two trams:
one tram, perhaps,
and one quill pen.
Or if two –
two swans
softly skimming the river's surface
as if by stealth;
nudging Avon's banks
in their gentle progress;
elegantly escorting the Countess
and her carousers
till she chugs noisily away,
leaving them
to shelter in the whispering reeds,
then glide effortlessly
through the hanging mist,
together
into the golden twilight.

Neil Zoladkiewicz

Interlude – Port d'Andratx

Cormorant, charcoal plumage
shining emerald and sapphire lights,
stretches his neck, spreads wings,
absorbs heat.
He occupies his favourite perch
on the quay's edge,
a statue with closed eyes
day-dreaming his time off
as we, so close,
sip chilled white wine,
tilt heads back, spread arms
in delicious worship of warmth.
The seascape deepens,
green, turquoise, magenta,
reflecting the sky's secret colours.
Small fish shoal unaware,
swim sinuous circles,
shadows following through shallows
on pale sand.
Sparrows crumb decking around us.
White sails laze across the estuary,
slip silently into the marina.
Time for lunch. *We* order;
he tenses, launches himself,
floats, still, quiet …
dives, an underwater arrowhead,
multi-coloured missile
showing off his hunting skills
a fathom below our feet.

Hilary Tinsley

from the walls of Chicago Library

she borrowed quotes

Tuesday was Lincoln Park
flight and room good
up early for walk
hope you like the postcards
what do you think of this
Libraries are the evidence
Of hope for the future
I've cut it a bit
I've cut T S Eliot

Wednesday was the Navy Pier
been walking for hours
just had cocktail
who is David McCullough
What journeys of mind and spirit
Are there for the taking with a library card
or a notebook and pencil

Thursday was the History Museum
I'm late for the ballet
Libraries keep the records
On behalf of all humanity
that was Varton Gregarian
you'll have to look him up as well

Friday was Willis Tower
back tomorrow
Getting my library card was like citizenship
It was like American citizenship
Oprah Winfrey – a woman at last

Saturday was O'Hare
scribbling in queue
hope I can post this
Libraries share all of our senses
that was me
what do you think
see you Friday
put the kettle on.

Terry Quinn

Fifty: A Theory of Significant Numbers

The numbers we crown
with precious metals and gems
are accidents
of history and anatomy.
Had Babylon triumphed,
would dozens have displaced decades?
Were we mitten-handed,
would bronze, silver, gold
be four, sixteen, sixty-four?
Starfish, too, might favour five
and squid share our delight in tens.
But, perhaps, insects celebrate
each six hours of life
and wolves howl in awe
at the five hundred and twelves of stars
surrounding the moon.

Catherine Fitzsimons

Journey

Watery fields, a flicker of sunlight
return me to farmland,
to flat summer days

through deeps, into shallows
to wade in the brook,
sweep carefree through corn;
to dry seasons, high seasons,
blue and mellow,
to plough and furrow.

Breezy flap, shadowed rain
torments the ragged smock on a stick.
A tractor scatters the mocking crows.
Chug and caw. Chug and caw.

Map rivers, clear as
veins on a trembling hand
show me wisdom
and wistfulness,

remind me I'm held
by your reasoning still.
I am whom you set going;
your gentle push
almost prepared me for this.

No parting waters to guide me home;
just winter fields,
watery,
but changed.

Dorothy Nelson

Time Preserved

We waited until mid-winter
to open the jar,
the one we'd carefully
wrapped in our beach towel
and placed in our suitcase.

It survived the flight home,
didn't shatter,
wasn't confiscated at customs
and for months afterwards
it sat at the back
of our kitchen cupboard,
waiting.

On a day in January
when endless spiteful rain fell,
we retrieved our treasure.
The glass bore no label,
the viscous amber sweetness
contained within described itself.

Anticipation tremored
as we opened the lid:
bending forward we inhaled
aroma of a Kefalonian July;
sweet, thyme suffused, honey:
we tasted, we kissed
and Ionian heat ran liquid on our lips.

Stephen Beattie

Understudy

I bow and revel in rapturous applause.
It is time to bask in the limelight at last,
a triumph after years of having to exist
hidden in the shadow of my elder sister.
She was always the apple of my parents' eyes,
my birth just an inconvenient accident.

She attended stage school every week,
though Dad was redundant and times were hard.
My only diversion was a newspaper round,
my prized possession her hand-me-down watch.
She swanned off to college to study theatre.
I took a job in an office and lived in austerity.

I went into amdram when she went on tour,
'a star in the making' the local rag claimed.
We met three years later at an audition
for the female lead in a West End bound show.
Her charm and experience won her the part
while my talent cast me as her understudy.

The show was a smash on the opening night,
followed by a party in the writer's flat.
She was the one they all gathered around,
happily drunk on adulation and booze.
I merged into a corner in lonely resentment,
till the sycophants started to drift away.

She swayed onto the balcony for a breath of air
but a four storey plunge proved the death of her.
So now I'm the star with greatness ahead,
my big break when the hand of fate intervened.
Well actually it wasn't fate's hand, but mine,
the one next to my stylish brand new Gucci watch.

Mike Cracknell

Stick gathering at Golitha Falls

If every stick or stone
in my bag and boot
on this unexceptional day
had a walk attached
all valley tied, fell studded
plain or plimsoll,
even barefoot tired,
I would have enough.
They would be my wood,
my hedge and beach,
my cottage hearth beside,
each one turned
and seasoned by a hand,
a paw, a storm,
a child or tide;
a better gathering tied
under the chiselled hazel
lintel of my heart
unbriared.

Dawn Bauling

All in a Day's Work

I didn't close my eyes the first time,
not like some of them,
I just aimed for the heart.

I've never fired the blank,
I'd know, the recoil feels different
coughing out a bit of wadding

instead of something lethal.
Now I hunt men.
When I see one I aim; hold my breath,

not for too long or the rifle shakes,
squeeze the trigger and
the head explodes.

I'm compassionate.
Some of them aim low
so it's long and lingering.

But I like it,
         Quick,
             Clean,
                  Nice.

John Mills

Stone Sofas of West Nab

Dark crags and boulders are Atlases
starkly shouldering the lowering sky.
You can hear their groans on the wind,
        mingled with the ghost cry of the lapwing.

The stone sofas on Meltham Moor
gather rain in their abandoned seats.
Once granite giants sat watch over the dark landscape,
till dawn sent them striding back
beneath the earth to their peat caverns
in carboniferous valhallas
        under the high swell of the moors.

Perhaps once Moai and Colossi came from distant lands,
swilled dark beer from Millstone cups,
and sang the world into being with their Pennine cousins.
But things turned uncordial at midnight, and in a drunken spat,
rocks got hurled and scattered.
Then the stone cock crowed on the Cock Crowing Stone
in that dawn of time.
        All turned to Millstone Grit, all petrified.

The landscape is the story
and the meaning.
I merely wander across
like a miniature figure in a Chinese painting,
– already a lost strand of narrative
        in its mythic geology.

Mary Lister

When

As she waved goodbye
I could feel the tears
Running down my face.
I will miss her smile,
Her company;
Her infectious laughter.
I do not know
When I will see her again.
We are isolated –
From our family and friends.
Isolated, from life
As we know it.
We face an uncertain future.
Will life ever be
The same again?
Questions, with no answers.
So we take one step,
And one day at a time.
Waiting to pick up
Our lives and freedom.
When, we do not know.

Sue Brotherstone

Cobbles and Comfort

Shannon guides us around the studios,
behind the scenes and on set.
Amongst the hallowed props
are Ena Sharples' hairnet, Deidre Barlow's specs
and Hayley Cropper's eco-friendly coffin;
iconic costumes – Bet Lynch's leopardskin,
Roy Cropper's bag
and Annie Walker's Mayoral chain.

We progress to the Rovers Return
where we pull an imaginary pint,
then emerge on to the street via the doors
marked Ladies and Gents in the pub.
We are in adult Disneyworld wandering
past the Kabin, Kevin Webster's garage
and other familiar landmarks in the legendary street,
mother and daughter enjoying a walk through history.

Reluctantly we leave this little world
which portrays an aspect of society today,
and walk on to the real streets of Salford.
Building projects surround us; the evening sun
bouncing off glass and steel
causes uncomfortable glare and a degree of shock.

This is the new world moving into the future.
No familiarity or affinity here.
Mentally, I cling to the cobbles
and the comfort of the past.

Julie Boydell

Song of Summer

Long hours ago, long days, long and forgotten dreams
that resurrect themselves in summer night
when all the oak is washed in moonlight streams
and the cicada's song is old and slight.
Each year the season makes its rules again –
there will be loveliness, there will be peace,
there will be memories that give us pain
when longer nights reach zenith and decrease.
Each week the reckoning is slower-paced
that counts our apples picked or kisses shared;
each day the thought of sunset rest is laced
with more regret, as for a danger shared.

We hum again the endless locust's drone
for hours and days and dreams we thought were gone.

Amy Jo Schoonover

Anglers

Silent, intent on the dream
of a white-gold flash beneath them,
the anglers tip their thoughts out
like the wriggling bait
on the sodden dark earth.

Vacancy drifts on the wind,
past the hillock where pipers whoop.
I walk past the potato fields,
this stillness almost pushing me,
and I am jealous, as I fish for
metaphors to beat the last one.

Stephen Wade

Cardiosophy

You think sheep's heart from Redman's Butchers
for dissecting in Biology; a trail of pipes,
a glisten of purple muscle.

I think love hearts, pastel pink, violet;
be my valentine piped in red;
a bitter February day, scouring sweet shops.

You study four chambers – atria and ventricles –
pumping out bright arterial blood;
embracing its dark venous return.

I picture the necklaces we both wore;
two halves of a heart, together a perfect whole:
forever, ever friends.

Forget Galen. Think Harvey:
circulation is a figure of eight,
the heart at its core: infinity.

I dream first love – a bird fluttering
against the ribs of its cage.
JSB = MDP engraved on a sycamore.

You diagnose cyanotic disease;
heart sick, a failing organ missing a chamber,
or aortic stenosis – stone heart.

I believe the lore of Ancient Egypt:
after death a man's worth is measured
by balancing his heart with a feather.

Margaret Gleave

What Will They Give You?

What will they give you,
my darling baby boy –
so early this dark morning?

Will they give you seven candles
to guide you through the night?

Will they give you loaves and fishes
and water sweet as wine?

Will they give you a boat
that can ride through the storm?

What will they give you,
my darling baby boy –
so early this dark morning?

Will they give you a purse
filled with silver gleaming bright?

Will they give you a tree
dressed in berries cold and white?

Will they give you a kiss
in a garden before dawn?

What will they give you,
my darling baby boy?

Will they give you
a crown of thorns?

Dave Ward

The Cuttings

On all my rail journeys out from Lime Street
I've never missed the cuttings
never failed to be excited
by the dark high walls
the blackened sandstone
bedrock of the city, cut into
blasted, shaped by nineteenth century
enterprise. Steam, diesel, electric:
countless trains have slipped out
through these tall passes,
with human freight
each to an individual fate.

And mine: child pleasures first
bound for the London adventure,
secure in parents and a sense of history.
Later, the sad leavetakings,
aware now of personal destiny
the inevitable passage of each of us alone
out through a dark gorge.

                    Gladys Mary Coles

An Amazonian Outing

I miss those winceyette warm mornings
when toes, still round from lack of use,
pattered outside my bedroom door,
while I feigned sleep.

I felt their kisses, like moths
dusting my skin; masked demands
to offer up the slightest sound
to show that I'm awake.

All hope of slumber lost,
my head became a stepping stone
to Jack-tars disguised as cherubs
wanting to set sail at first light!

Captain chosen, then first mate,
the crew, a mongrel mix of teddies,
sailed boldly down the Amazon
with pencils serving as blowpipes.

We rowed over rapids, saw crocs playing lego,
rescued a gorilla with loose stuffing,
when a voice far below the water line
called 'pancakes!' Then everyone jumped ship.

Carol Blanche Featherstone

The Smell of Creosote

It was deep country then, the Essex-Hertford border.
Bus, even in the 50's, once a week.
The cottage – was it actually thatched?
Why they chose it for retirement I can't now reconstruct.
For Grandad was a townsman, a West Londoner,
though, carpenter by trade, most definitely
a capable townsman, with a splendid white moustache.
But Granny, who had been in service, long before
was born a country girl. I was embarrassed
at how she used to click ill-fitting dentures,
but she taught me what words the wood dove says.
I was a child of seven or eight. What did I know
of adult dreams? I didn't know they had them..
Memory tatters. Fragments survive.
Sleeping in the little room in comfort under the rafters,
I read precociously the magazines they left me.
Nothing else of the interior remains.
But this is clear:
The rounded whitewashed stones that lined the path.
The smell of creosote on the wooden fence.

                    Colin H.E. Wiltshire

Anderby Creek

Someone is calling
his name, a faint voice
lost in a strange
perplexing roar.
He wonders if he's
back in the car
on the concrete road
before the window
clicked and locked.

Shadows crack and burn.
Eyes focus
on a glittering beach,
the slavering sea
close, and loud, its jaws
opening and closing.

A line of boys and girls
stands still before it,
skewered to the sand,
their turned backs
precisely done,
speckled with salt.

Hidden forces heft
a cathedral of sea.
Lateral trails unfurl.
Foam flickers, gushes
out of sabre teeth.

Something won't let go.
Jerking round, he's
confronted by his mother's
concerned face,
her lips moving.

Now he's at her side,
walking away, the bank
blocking his view.

Would you like an ice cream?
He can hear her now.

Martin Domleo

Grandad's Garden

I turn the cone upside down,
it changes to a flower,
like the dahlias
in Grandad's garden
where creepy earwigs
hide inside.

I paint my pinecone fiery orange,
use a green-striped straw for the stem,

wrap it in mistletoe paper,
place it under the tree
as a special present
for Mummy
on Christmas Day,

to make her smile,
cos she cries in bed, every night,
since Grandad died.

Patricia M Osborne

Evening Sheep

Shaped like summer clouds, they float
in fading light,
where, drizzle-dipped, they graze
their weight of night,
starlight, moon, their heads
bent into a tide
of November haze.

Their parents will have grazed
and ancestors before them
up and down these fields
over centuries
stunned by snow and wind,
their footsteps, memories
written in the land.

They seem to dwell in dream,
moving, halting, still,
sometimes looking up
with that blind gaze,
like seeking something lost
that they forgot
as we forget a name.

Some of them migrate
in and out of dips
through shadows, deep
into shallow light,
almost winter light
like walking into sleep.

Irene Thomas

The Little Wood

There's always a little wood somewhere
Where you think of what lies ahead:
Meeting the hostile client;

Chairing the difficult Board;
Breaking the dreadful news.
You wonder how you got here,

When almost anyone you've ever known
Would do a better job; you think
How very much you'd like to get away.

In the wood, you seem to have a choice.
Briefly you're Machiavelli.
Strategic illness beckons.

In the little wood you learn the cost,
And why you're there. And who
You are. And what, in fact, you'll do.

R. V. Bailey

Mr Phoebus at Mordiford

Here comes Elgar on his upright Sunbeam,
pumping the pedals from Plâs Gwyn trimly
to Tarrington and Trumpet via Bagpiper's Tump.
He dismounts a moment at Mordiford Bridge
to listen to the lithic lisp of the water,
the swills and spills,
the mad quadrilles,
the weary wind of the wandering Lugg.

He fancies he sees Ophelia floating,
deadly, dreamy, dimity nightshade,
slippery stave of quavering streamers,
weed-clad willowy wand of youth,
with every elver and every eddy
washing unfinished works away.

He notes the rhythm of the riddling river,
whose trio of triple-tongued tell-tale goddesses,
long since lost in the land of the fathers,
watched once over the Y of the Wye,
and he wonders whether he will still hear
his westward muse,
or will she choose
to hang up her Hereford harp when he leaves?

He eyes a brace of easy anglers,
rods and reels and ringing wet silence,
cuts a cidered slipshod squaredance,
climbs aboard the cranky, creaking
Mr Phoebus, fashioning fragments,
and hums Hello to Hampstead Heath.

                    Peter Sutton

Iceland: Fire and Freeze

Shadows ride Viking horses
on glacial planes untrodden by man.
Basalt pillars rise at Dimmuborgir;
Satan's dwelling when cast from heaven.

I sip Brennivín and lemon, lounging
in ice-blue geysers steam-fed
by sulphurous cauldrons
boiling the blood of a fractured land.

Bad-egg breath chars tundra yellow,
latitude freezes waterfalls dead
as arctic elves dance the northern skies
green, to the backdrop of snow-robed peaks.

Francesca Hunt

Lockdown 1: The Song of Silence

It was the birdsong residents noticed first.
Its presence penetrated the still sky,
a new awakening, an early morning call.
Yet they had always been there,
high above the polluted air,
unable to compete with the roar of the dragons
and the fiery fumes filling their tiny lungs.
But just for a little while they were heard.
They made the most of it;
singing their hearts out in the silent suburbs.

Denise Randall

Putting My Affairs In Order

A friend has told me I should do this, just in case I die.
I've thought about it quite a lot, but still can't reason why
there is a need. She seemed insistent, so I'll have a try:

I've cast my mind back years: my first affair was with Joe
                                                        Green.
He liked to make love in the open but I wasn't keen.
Alfresco sex is not for me; what happens if you're *seen*?

The next one was a chap called Stan; now Stan was four foot
                                                        ten.
Although he was quite nice I really *do* like taller men,
and after several dates I thought, 'I won't see him again.'

I think that number three was . . . wait a minute . . . it was Bob.
He knew which buttons he should press, but wouldn't get a
                                                        job,
and so he had to go. The man was just a total slob.

Hang on, I may have got it wrong, and Bob was number four.
Or was it Charlie, Bruce or Steve? I really can't be sure.
This 'putting them in order' business really is a chore.

My next affair—where am I, up to seven? Oh yes, Jim,
a famous politician, so that name's a pseudonym.
He told me lies (yes, really!) so I very soon dumped him.

Before—or was it after?—that came Billy, on a cruise.
I don't remember much except we sank . . . a lot of booze.
He'd moan and sweat excessively when . . . taking off his
                                                        shoes!

Let's see, I hope I've got it right: Joe, Stan, Bob, Charlie,
                                                        Bruce,
then Steve and Jim and Billy; quite a few, but my excuse
is that I'm rather gullible, and easy to seduce.

Although I've done the sequence, my *dramatis personae*,
I still don't see the need to write this down before I die.
When one's 'affairs are all in order,' who d'you notify?

Jayne Osborn

Say it with Flowers

Thank you for this bunch of words
of freesia, phlox, fritillary,
pinks, petunias, peony,
lupin and lobelia,
daffodil and dahlia,
honeysuckle, honesty.

Each flower a word you cannot say,
but verbalised through this bouquet
of vibrant tender beauty.

Behind you, through the garden door
petal, sepal, stalk, stem, leaf,
dew damp daisy as the dawn
brushes the greenness of the lawn,
give us a dictionary of love,
speak to us of what you mean.

Susan Clark

Wild Rose

The wild rose nearly didn't bloom:
he screwed it up and filed it with the trash.
But mother retrieved it, smoothed it out
and saved it for a rainy day.
Mothers' judgements usually are
so much wiser than their sons'.
Mine was always two or three
steps ahead of me and knew
at one brief glance, whether to shame,
cajole, intimidate or praise.
At seven, I wanted desperately to play,
but like poor disillusioned Jude,
who thought there was a simple code
to turn his English into Latin,
I was convinced that in a year
I would be Chopin or Rachmaninoff.
All that was long ago and heaven knows
how many hours to master one wild rose.
I played it yesterday and marvelled
as I always do, that so much depth
could be expressed with such simplicity.
I sensed the woodland, smelled the scent
and touched the yellow velvet of the rose.
I thank our mothers for their confidence,
their tailored skills in moulding us:
his for fined-tuned musicality,
mine for instinct and tenacity.
Next time, I'll play the wild rose just for them.

Vince Smith

Kirkstall Abbey
For Beryl and Jennifer

There is power here among the ruins
As jackdaws 'chak' from above,
Power runs and threads
Through these remains.

Down the night stair
A sense of monks moving,
Lips and bodies synchronised
In praise. For them, no doubt,
Days would come when words seemed vapid,
God a lie, life devoid of hope –
Yet the Rule held. The discipline
Of year on year, sleeping and rising,
Has worn a thread through time
Up and down this stair.

So high the walls, and stout,
But dissolution came, violence
And destruction in the name of God.
Then the slow ruin of the years,
The crumbling and decay,
Indignity of highway through the nave,
Desecration of neglect
Year upon heedless year.

Now though, Kirkstall stands with grace –
Restoration's gift.
The jackdaws 'chak' and nest
As all their fore-birds did,
Pageants are held; visitors come to wonder and to learn,
Perhaps to sense the power of this place –
Kirkstall's legacy held in trust.

Ceinwen Sanderson

Doon the Watter fur the Fair

They daunder frae the boardin hoose
Oan tae the beach
Set up thir deckchairs.

Granpa rolls up his shirtsleeves tae the elba,
unbuttons his waistcoat, but keeps it oan,
folds up his trooser legs as far as his knees,
taks aff his shoes an soacks, knots his hanky
oan tae his heid.
An that's him.

Granma gies him a smile, slips aff her sandals,
rolls aff her stockins, carefully tooks her frock
in tae the legs o her bloomers, plonks a straw hat
oan tap o her perm, gies a model's shimmy,
juist fur effect.
An that's her.

Shadin their een frae sun skinklin oan sea
they heid doon fur a paidle.
Castin' aff thir inhibitions.

Fiona McFadzean

Contributor's note: I have added this one although it is in Scots
as it is relevant to Mal's roots. And very reminiscent of our
parents' generation when everyone went to the seaside 'doon
the watter' for the fair, The Glasgow Fair which was the
general holiday, first two weeks in July.

Bottom's Dream

We'd gone to the woods for a practice,
For we were performing at court.
I was Pyramus, the brave, noble hero
And acted superbly, I thought.

Then something peculiar happened:
My friends all ran screaming away.
And instead of a tankard of bitter,
I fancied a bundle of hay.

The queen of the fairies approached me –
A very attractive young lass –
But still I heard Peter Quince shouting,
'Oh Bottom, stop playing the ass!'

My memory's now somewhat hazy…
I lay on a bank of sweet flowers.
Titania stroked me and kissed me –
The canoodling went on for hours!

Then I woke on the cold ground at cockcrow,
Back to normal, or so it would seem.
So was it a fling with a fairy
Or just a midsummer night's dream?

Elizabeth Horrocks

No Day Returns

From this place of parting and departure
See curvature of steel slice out of sight,
Suggesting static speed, fast frozen flight.
Scimitar shapes, dissecting distances,
Permanent way to sever local love.
Permanent way, transient travellers,
Timetabled traffic, burrowing bridges,
Carving through cuttings, slamming through stations,
Along embankments where wild flowers wave.
My train of thought tracks back through space and time
Recalling holidays of other days,
Smokey and steamy journeys to the sea,
Sunshine on sand and orgies of ice cream,
Arrivals and departures in brown barometered hallways
Of sundry Sunnyhaven or Sea view.
Later journeys, visits to far places,
Recall obscure, the reasons obsolete.
I reset all the pivot points of change
Arriving always at the here and now.
Now, I will wait no more beneath the clock,
Reunion half hoped for overdue,
Presume permanent parting of the way.
On this journey it seems, no day returns.

Mike Rathbone

The Torrent of Time

From wild and lonely moorland fell
Where ptarmigan and pheasant dwell,
I slowly make my long descent
Past mighty Whernside, Pen-y-Ghent
And Ingleborough's levelled top
Through weathered limestone crags, I drop;
Beneath which, men climb down to find
Formations I have left behind –
The Organ and the Angel tied
Against the rock-face, petrified.
And nearby, spanning rolling hills
That snaking viaduct, which takes
The train from Yorkshire to the Lakes.

Historic Clitheroe has spas
Still filled from Stygian depths of ours;
And yet I spill remorselessly
Along the valley to the sea.
Past Ribchester, where locals say
The Roman cohorts make their way
Along the ancient road; each ghost
In ordered route march to the coast,
To poor, proud Preston, where time mocks
Once busy, now redundant docks.

From hill-top source to Irish Sea
The Ribble marks our history.

Yvonne M. Fee

Misunderstanding

Birdsong filled the garden
as alchemical syrinxes transmuted base breath into
golden notes spil
      l
       i
         n
          g
            from golden bills
We listened almost reverently to nature's beauty.

We heard
a mellifluous euphony
a melodious duet
that damsel with a dulcimer in distant Xanadu.
We saw
a team, a twosome, a duo
working together
affirming, confirming
a whole, a totality
as from opposite bushes
azalea and yew

they sang *at* each other

Each singing
for dominance
for territory
for a mate
      competing
          squabbling
    fighting

The world is not always what it seems.

Andy Williams

Respect

Mole – that's me. Or, if you prefer,
Mouldywarp – dirt tosser – my name
from time out of mind. Respect me.
I am King of Crumble, and Lord of Loam:
my lifetime will be spent in the service of soil.

Earth is my obsession. Respect that.
Always I feel it flaked between my claws:
clods cling to my pallid palms.
Shovel-like, they are purpose built.

Relinquishing sight long ago,
I evolved an underground sat nav
second to none, am able to divine
the nearness of worms or infinitesimal
shifts of air where there is no air.
Worms respect me – fearful
of my paralysing saliva, of imprisonment
in my living larder. A neat touch,
don't you think?

Day and night do not exist
for me, though I relish the comfort
of snuggling into dirt-dark duvets,
and will snooze happily under eiderdowns
of earth, or counterpanes of clay.

Above ground affairs don't concern me,
nor company entice me. Being alone suits me.
It's unlikely, but should you encounter a group of us,
we prefer to be addressed as 'a labour of moles' –
an appropriate acknowledgement of our industry.
A mark of respect, you might say.

Corinne Lawrence

Broken

'All your favourite biscuits just a little bit broken
Snuggled together in a big family sized box.'

In Woolworths you could
Buy them by the quarter pound.
The assistant would scoop
And shovel them into a brown
Paper bag:
An avalanche of chance,
A gamble of confectionery.

As a child I would try
To match them up,
Make them whole again,
Broken circles,
Split wafers,
Custard creams
With the corners missing.

There were always a few
That never found their match,
Oddments too small
Left to crumble
Like lumpy sand
At the bottom of the barrel.

Is it possible to be
Just a *little bit* broken?
Can fragments *snuggle together*
In a mismatch of shape and size?
Edges cannot help but catch and clash.

Still, I struggle to put the damaged
Pieces of my life back together,
Wonder why they will not fit.

Jacqueline Woods

Branwen … Before, and Later.

Glossy white feathers
catch emerald iridescence from the Sun
as she soars over London.
White raven spirit, Branwen, goddess of love,
is summoned, unlocked, from the Celtic underworld,
by her new-named namesake, the little Raven-girl.
She alights on the White tower.
Her brother Bran's head was buried far below,
beneath the White Mound, in Bronze age legend,
to keep dead-eyed watch over all Britain.

Now, in soft-plumed fluttering
Branwen flies down to her dark Raven-child,
strokes her glossy down, her midnight feathers,
and the small keen beak, not yet come into its full 'Caw'.
The little eyes blink at her radiance.
Her power transmits.
Rightfully named among ravens, little Branwen,
night-winged spirit of the forest, descended
down through the Mabinogion,
will watch over London
out-blinking Domesday.

Mary Lister

The Crich Tram

Ten tons of wood and steel for just ten pounds;
the price to pay to stay the breaker's hand.
Our city streets no longer ring with sounds
of wheel on rail, for buses rule the land.

Bright-painted tramcars, rarely to be seen
in English towns, climb high through Derby hills.
The grime where once they worked replaced by green,
the workers' transport now gives tourist thrills.

Malcolm Chisholm

The Shed

The Shed is ...

where a man can always find what he needs,
where he does real work, not jobs around the house,
where 'things that will come in handy' remain forever,
where he can lose himself, but his wife can always find him,
where the beer fridge lives,
where he finds real peace and quiet,
where he has mid-life ... without the crisis.

Malcolm Chisholm

When Did we Last?

I cannot recall the last time
I skipped instead of walked,
took our girls to the park to play on swings,
went shopping with my mother –
and through unspecified aches and age and death,
none can be repeated now.

This is why I treat every day
as the last day of the rest of my life,
relish the bus into town
I might never catch again,
close and caress the favourite book
I may never re-open,
note every shift and shade
of sunset's incandescence.

There is no drama in forgetting,
no credit in remembering –
and yet
when the lights go out
I conspire with you to make sure
I love you is the last thing I say;
I love you is the last thing I hear.

Alison Chisholm

Moving On

Beside a river, by a rock,
I picture you stumbling across
stepping stones and looking
at me as though you found it
not so much fun.

Yet you persevered,
wanting to prove that even at
your age you could make it
without falling in or needing
any help from me.

I waited patiently for you –
took pictures, smiled at your
determination, and when you
finally made it to the other side,
we moved on.

Annette Heys

Beached Jellyfish

This near-transparent plodge stranded
at sea's lip is an upturned Lalique platter,
its centre the smoky-blue of water-thinned milk
set in an haloed rim, clearer and as cold
as glass but rubbery, with the littlest of give
as if resisting inroads.

And yet, it's no way collectible,
this reckoning of negation
that possesses no visible inner machinery;
no twitching lymph; no blood, no skin, no face;
nothing that resembles an eye or ear.
And no response when prodded;
though it gives a squish and sluck
when eased with nudging Croc or stick.

Keeping it alive's the tricky thing.
Too massy by half for kid's plastic spade,
it's slippery-difficult in lifting – slides
over the side, collapsing flatly, and
splatting on sand. And mustn't touch
with hand or foot. So best to leave it
islanded there, kept wet by deepings
of beach-bucketed sea.

Then, if it survives till the turn of tide,
this *Medusa* will meld with the pulsing shunt
and push of its trailing veils
into a full-moon face
ghosting through prehistory's galaxy.

But, for the now, herring-gulls are gathering.

Roger Elkin

Christmas in Wales

In 1938 we spent Christmas at the Grapes Hotel in Llangollen.
On Christmas Eve I lay and listened to the great iron bunch of
grapes
Swinging and creaking in the wind,
Hoped for sleigh bells and tried to sleep.

And after stocking time and presents,
On a frost bright Christmas morning
We climbed Dinas Bran,
Looked down upon the toy sized town,
And heard the curlews call.

Then with brisk appetites
We scrambled back for dinner,
Roast turkey and pudding with a silver sixpence.
There was a children's party later,
Crackers and noisy games.
I felt lonely, longed to leave.

For what I really loved
Was sitting in the lounge,
Sipping lime juice with a swoosh of soda water,
And listening in to adult conversation.
One little group particularly fascinated.

High posh voices rang across the room,
'Two gin and Its Gareth, a martini,
(Don't forget the cherry), and a double whiskey.'
The ladies crossed their silk clad legs,
(I loved their pretty shoes),
Flicked ash from cigarettes,
And talked of dances, parties, whist and bridge,
And someone called Monty Carlo.

'I had such ghastly cards darling,
No luck at all. Lorst a packet,
Jack was *furious*!'
'Oh drown your sorrows sweetie,
Another brandy? Merry Christmas!'
I savoured every word.

And back at home my best friend Jean and I
Put a jug of water on a tray,
Two empty potted meat jars served as glasses,
Rolled up paper for our cigarettes.
'G and T darling or martini?' I said.
'Oh martini and two cherries please.'
Jean was quick to learn.
'Did you go to Gerald's party?'

'Yes … the usual damn shambles.
Beryl looked an absolute fright!'
'Well, chin chin my sweet.'
We clinked the little pots.

A well known sniff was heard.
My Grandma entered like the wrath of God.
Teetotal to her fingertips,
She was appalled at such debauchery.

'Swearing! Drinking! Disgusting!'
She poured our drinks back in the jug.
'Only water Gran,' I said.
She fixed me with her eyes.
'Why can't you play some nice and wholesome games?'

Jean said, 'I think my mum's expecting me.'
I fetched her coat,
There was no point in asking her to stay.
We couldn't think of any wholesome games.

Shirley Tomlinson

They said they would take me to Keswick

They said they would take me to Keswick,
That it sure wouldn't be any bother –
Now I've two barm cakes sticking down one ear...
And a pan handle stuck down the other.

I'm wearing a mac and three cardies,
I've four stinky boots on my lap,
A duvet is draped like a shawl round my neck
While perched on my head's a flat cap.

I'm wedged in between a slow cooker,
With knobs pressing into my hips,
And a kettle, four mugs, and a fryer, deep fat,
In case we should fancy some chips.

But, though I'm shoehorned in one corner
(With an increasing need for the loo),
Towns are surrendering to snow covered peaks
And I'm *perfectly* placed for the view!

I'm *delighted* they've brought me to Keswick,
So when they've untangled my legs,
I'll embrace the self catering spirit
And make us all bacon and eggs!

                    Marian Cleworth

Lessons from an Orchard

Long weeks ago I brought this apple home,
a ripe and shining present from a friend.

It rested on the table fresh and green;
white rings today decorate brown skin.

Since there is no obvious sign of rot
even now I cannot throw it out.

Light as locks of hair when picked up
the underside is like a contoured map,

ridges, gulleys mark a dark terrain;
the whole has shrunk to less than half its size.

Closely guarded on my study shelf
it brings to mind Oscar's masterpiece.

How much am I in the decomposing fruit?
Has any part, a pip perhaps, stayed good?

I wonder why those rings have not coalesced
and need to know what will happen next.

It has taught me much, informing that
Schiller needed smell of apples to write,

kept them rotting in a drawer in his room.
This apple has become, for me, an icon.

Peggy Poole

Let's Not Go Out On This Winter Day

Let's not go out on this winter day,
the wind is shouting at the walls,
the fire won't take that long to catch,
the softness of the sofa calls.
Let's not go out on this winter day,
let's both hold still and think of ways
to travel worlds inside our heads,
refuse the places winter stays.
Let's walk through books, let's walk through poems,
visit Fern Hill and Dover Beach;
to Yeats' Lake Isle of lnnisfree,
Frost's America, Homer's Greece.
Let's drink too much and let's laugh too loud,
let's find what sheer indulgence brings;
let's clink our glasses while we can
and catch each other's hiccupping!
Then let our music resound from rooms,
as we struggle to sing as one;
Landslide, Forever Young,
Ruby Tuesday, Here Comes The Sun.
Let's not go out on this winter day
but well before the flames expire,
let's sink into each other's arms,
make love before our winter fire.

                    Ronnie Goodyer

Pie-eyed Wagtail

He has competed with a dozen drunken wasps
to sip the sweet cider;
downed a skinful
till his wings are good for nothing.

Under cover of the apple tree,
its branches an umbrella
for his befuddled head, he dozes,
leaning tight against the trunk.

When the first fat blobs of rain
bounce like a peppering of bullets
on the leaves above
and spill onto his chest,

he stirs, and lies back open-beaked,
eyes struggling to focus
on an upturned world of branches
swimming over him.

Swollen as a newly-risen leaf,
full-blown and far from home,
he lolls among the windfalls
singing rude songs.

Karen Pailing

Rising damp

'A river can sometimes be diverted, but it is a very hard thing to lose it altogether.' (J.G.Head: paper read to the Auctioneers' Institute in 1907)

At our feet they lie low,
The little fervent underground
Rivers of London

Effra, Graveney, Falcon, Quaggy,
Wandle, Walbrook, Tyburn, Fleet

Whose names are disfigured,
Frayed, effaced.

These are the Magogs that chewed the clay
To the basin that London nestles in.
These are the currents that chiselled the city,
That washed the clothes and turned the mills,
Where children drank and salmon swam
And wells were holy.

They have gone under.
Boxed, like the magician's assistant.
Buried alive in earth.
Forgotten, like the dead.

They return spectrally after heavy rain,
Confounding suburban gardens. They infiltrate
Chronic bronchitis statistics. A silken
Slur haunts dwellings by shrouded
Watercourses, and is taken
For the footing of the dead.

Being of our world, they will return
(Westbourne, caged at Sloane Square,
Will jack from his box),
Will deluge cellars, detonate manholes,
Plant effluent on our faces,
Sink the city.

Effra, Graveney, Falcon, Quaggy,
Wandle, Walbrook, Tyburn, Fleet

It is the other rivers that lie
Lower, that touch us only in dreams
That never surface. We feel their tug
As a dowser's rod bends to the source below

Phlegethon, Acheron, Lethe, Styx.

U. A. Fanthorpe

Bright Stars

Bold Lover, never, never canst thou kiss,
Though winning near the goal–yet, do not grieve;
She cannot fade, though thou hast not thy bliss,
For ever wilt thou love, and she be fair!
          John Keats, 'Ode on a Grecian Urn'

The evening falls. They sit, fingers entwined.
Many a year has died since they broke through
the fastness of cold glaze and, passion-blind,
secured that kiss. He tracks the waning blue
as best he can, his vision failing now.
She moves to gift her bones a touch more ease.
United by one thought, they ponder how
they cheated stasis, voyaged on living seas.

Do they regret it? Never. True, they found
that mortal love can play such merry hell
with heart, tongue, forehead. Now and then around
them brute existence wove the old, old spell:
hurt, pride, indifference. Yet here they are,
together still, still happy to be free
of priest, trussed heifer, pious morning star –
abandoned to that Attic potpourri.

She strokes his cheek. He smiles. The twilight spreads.
'Truth … Beauty,' they reflect. And shake their heads.

                    Michael W. Thomas

On Not Going to Skegness

No, I have never visited Skegness –
apparently such bracing wild North Sea,
and this omission pains me, I confess.

Do people ever go to convalesce?
It might be more effective than Torquay.
No, I have never visited Skegness.

I'm sure the town has plenty to impress,
and that the skies are open, wide and free
and this omission pains me, I confess,

though I have looked it up, for I possess
a guide book. But you can't go there to ski.
No, I have never visited Skegness.

I think I am beginning to obsess
about its vibe, its charms unknown to me,
and this omission pains me. I confess

to taking hols abroad with great success.
The east coast boring? No, I disagree!
But I have never visited Skegness
and this omission pains me, I confess.

Joyce Reed

Sunrise Concertante

Burnt golden rays break
the night-time sky,
beating on the Ouse's slow crawl.

Air-warmed sweet-grasses
fan fragrance into the wind:
marsh marigolds shine.

A blackbird's
chromatic glissando sweeps

towards the riverbank.

Swanking his red tuxedo, a robin
trills to join the recital

as elm silhouettes dance,
watching their mirror image.

The mistle thrush flaunts
his speckled belly. He takes his turn
to chant – introduces

hedge sparrows who chatter,
boast brown suits.

A cadenza call governs the concerto–
plump skylark makes his solo in the skies.

Shades of light peep,
geese chevron across the blue,
noses down, necks stretched, wings

spread wide. Honking their signal sound,
they climb the horizon and sky-fall
on to daylight's iridescent waves.

Patricia M Osborne

Christmas 1942

Scissors snipped and tongues licked.
Multi-coloured paper chains snaked the room.
Rolls of sticky paper, that criss-crossed windows
to stop bomb blast, made good decorations.
We had a turkey to pluck.
Feathers floated like snowflakes
around the kitchen.
It came from the 'Black Market'
Which intrigued me,
but our butcher wouldn't say
where I could find this place.

I hung my Christmas socks
over the bed rail by my gas mask,
and wondered as I snuggled down
how Father Christmas would find us
in the black-out, or whether his reindeers
would get tangled up in the cables
from the barrage balloons.
How brave he is, I thought.
He might meet a German plane
or get shot by one of ours.

I was so excited when I saw
my bulging socks and parcels next morning.

He was obviously given safe passage.
My elder brother was home on leave.
His ship had come in with food.
We had tinned pears and peaches
in our trifle – a special treat.
The boys' present to me was a jigsaw
of a battleship.
It was really for them to work on
but everyone sat fitting it together.

Mostly we were glad to be there,
all six of us clustered round the wireless
to listen to the King's speech
and his reassuring message,
that peace would come.

Dylys Osborne

Four O'Clock Fantasy

I look at you with lust, – so smooth and long,
Firm and cream-filled, yet softening to my tongue,
Your sleek, smooth covering heaven to my eyes.
My conscience pricks. I know I am unwise.

Your sensuous shapeliness invades my soul
With urgent passion to consume you, whole.
In my desire to press you to my lips
I feel you slinking slowly to my hips.

It breaks my heart to leave you lying there …
'Yes – How much is that chocolate eclair?'

Yvonne M. Fee

Forest Fox

He sensed my hesitation, untangled
my thoughts, disappeared before the sound
of heartbeat crossed the clearing.
Why do foxes think they're God's gift?

I followed, felt the ground give, squelch
of boots in mud and moss, heard the crack
of twigs as I plodded after him. He scampered
away, called me on, barked my name.

The rain came so cold it scorched
my cheeks and still the fox howled onwards,
turned his head towards me as he fox-trotted
through the fist of the forest.

On till gloom became darkness. We stopped.
He faced me. His drowned eyes stared
as he nosed the air; his coat was frost,
his mouth spit and steam.

I crouched to within a sniff of his face,
dared to ask, 'Do you believe …
and who will remember you when you die?'
'It's not about belief,' he said.

I reached and touched his head, felt slicked down
crisp fur, saw that fox as I would never
again. Then he licked me, turned, bounded off,
faded into the thick morning mist.

                    Peter Phillips

Young Turner at Brentford

He stands beside the river at tide-turn
seduced by water and by light.
He notes dark currents patterning the flow,
a Thames barge curving out of sight.

He sees the sun's thin rays threading through cloud,
a ferryman trimming his boat,
an osier-gatherer pleating basket-ware,
dull-surfaced buttons on a coat.

Then intermittent rain puddles the bank
and smudges colours palette grey.
He cannot sketch, except within his mind,
stores there impressions of the day.

He skims flat stones, watching their circled fall,
and gathers more, marking their sheen.
He feels their wetness, smoothness, in his hands,
and pockets some to paint pristine.

St. Lawrence tower's thin peal reminds the hour.
He slips around the market crush
for Mr. Lees' *Antiquities* awaits
more colour washes from his brush.

Tinting its plates with yellows, blues and greens,
with pinks and reds, flat tones for trees,
does his subconscious incubate ideas
to synthesise art's mysteries?

Is mist already traced with single hair
and colour leap in sunrise flame?
Does clarity of pictured moon presage
the luminosity of fame?

Beryl Cross

Time On His Hands

Outside the taverna, in the late afternoon
he sits at a plastic table,
lit by a shaft of sunlight.
Slowly, he wipes the thick, black,
clinging coffee stains
from his full white beard
with the back of the hand
that clutches the amber beads.

His other hand wonders whether
to pour a drop of clean water
into the glass of untouched ouzo
that waits on the table
next to the coffee cup;
whether to ignore the clock
and light another cigarette
before he starts to wander back

past white walls
warmed by the same sun
that shed its radiant light on Plato.

Bill Lythgoe

Pavement Artist

I see it now …
Paris in December,
turbulent with tourists near the Eiffel Tower.
He sprang into our path,
as I remember,
pulled on your sleeve,
'Can I draw you … please … first one of the hour?'
'What … ?' you spluttered,
while I said, 'How much?'
mouth set,
driving a hard bargain.
Then he cartooned you, with the artist's touch,
in charcoal strokes,
rapid and grey,
flowing like the Seine,
while I sat on the wall and laughed,
freezing
and shivering
in the silver rain.

                    Marian Cleworth

Phoenix

Rumours abound
concerning my birth,
no conventional hatching for me.
Fire was my mother, my father,
my all. I am not of the earth,
or of water or air.

I know nothing
of the last incarnation,
I'm only aware
when my time draws near,
I must prepare to die
and be born.

I fashion a nest
of cinnamon sticks, fragrant
with nutmeg, turmeric, cloves.
I sound my chant, turn
towards the sun, and beat
my purple wings.

The nest is alight,
I try to shut out the sound –
cracking, hissing, the stench
of burning feather and flesh.
I am consumed,
reduced to a fine white dust.

But inside the ashes
I feel life returning.
I regain solid form, feel
such infinite strength.
Flames lick my wings, I wrench
into flight, screeching joy,
in the cool blue of the sky.

                    Shelagh MacKinnon

Not Forgetting Grandad

He never opened my presents
till later. Knew they were tobacco
or socks. Until the day I returned
from a field course in Callander,
brought a small packet
neatly sealed in tartan paper
by the lady in the gift shop.
He shook it, couldn't guess,
tore the wrapper there and then.
A miniature whisky, tiny bottle,
tiny box. A Present from Scotland.
I saw him actually grin.

Hilary Tinsley

First Memory

Awaking from darkness
to a heavy bass rumbling,
the floor alive under him,
he rushed outside,
stumbling after older boys,
they, shouting one word:
'Tanks!' In raw excitement,
racing to the main road,
shouting again and again,
'Tanks!'

What were *tanks*?
What was anything?
He was two and a half,
knew nothing beyond sensation,
his mother's cradling.
Nothing to make a picture of,
before the tanks
came grinding,
heading for D Day
and God knows what.

Later, much later,
he wondered why *tanks*
came first among memories.

Then, he realised, they didn't.
It was the *running*,
the trying to keep up;
textures in stone and tar
rising and falling,
his brothers' cries
hauling him on elastic rope
towards the main road,
where undefined shapes,
great power and noise,
ghosted into dreams.

                    Martin Domleo

The Bench

Across the road and through the copse,
then up the rise to where the fence
is broken down.
The tops of bushes, each one dense
with diamante webs,
now shade what used to be the rec.,
I'm told, thanks to some lottery aid,
is soon to be a rest home for the old.
But look! The bench where we once met
and laughed and cried,
is standing yet.

It's broken, green with mildew but
the back, where our two names are carved,
is still intact and if I shut my eyes,
I see us, wrapped and scarved
and holding hands.
Our misted breath that rose
beneath a gibbous moon,
made promises of love till death.
That spectre took you far too soon
but this old bench where we once met,
and laughed and loved and cried,
is standing yet.

                              Dennis Bryant

The Loneliness of Snowmen

You made me what I am,
I stand with heavy middled pose,
a perch for blackbirds, robins;
a borrower of hat and scarf,
an old clay pipe and nose.

A dull shaped garden sentry,
I watch, as silent as the night,
frosted like the winter sky,
lit up by gems of frozen stars
and moon of silver light.

But at dawn, when sunlight
sends ice shards dripping, dripping;
it tilts my hat, my carrot nose,
my pipe and scarf all follow me
earthwards, slipping, slipping.

Unconcerned that I have gone,
you look skywards in suspense,
as giant settling flakes arrive
you start to build another me,
all white and innocence.

Gill Hawkins

Moon Rise Again

We come and go
like stars twinkling,

meet and retreat
like sea on the strand.

Restless, unseen
love flies in the wind.

Moon rise again
another month gone.

Shadows of night
quietly kissing,

daylight that comes
with nobody there.

Coffees in cafes
walks in the green woods,

sit by the sea
listening to words.

Talking of things
politics, music,

deaths of our friends
new babies that come.

Parents that age
grant forms and finance,

what exam marks
universities?

Driving around
timetabled journeys,

catch up at lunch
perhaps a quick stroll.

Meetings readings,
try to write poems.

Full moon again
twenty eight days gone.

Lucinda Carey

Summer Rain

We walk on the shoreline, recalling summer,
the laughter and meals outdoors, sipping wine slowly
then linking arms down seaside promenades.
The air is silk and all the days dancing.

Deckchairs on shingled beaches, music of waves
and sunlight reflected, stinging our eyes;
cold drinks and ice-creams, picnics
and summer rain, gentle like memories.

Doris Corti

A Tree in Dawlish

After the white flame of the snow
    consuming the black and grey
of footpath and road a dull time
    of wet and cold.
But now every tree flaunts its particular leaf;
    and the sun, some days at least
is so warm on bare legs and on shoulders
    that need no anorak or jumper.
I sit on a bench by bright water flowing
    and ponder the unified
yet twisted shape of one tree
    in particular. Today
I feel surrounded by the old.
    They pass me chattering
of the odd doings of grandchildren;
    or walking their dogs
and having canine orientated conversations
    with other owners
of highly individual and cantankerous animals.
    So why do I
who am not so vastly different in age
    sit here and worry
about the shape of a particular tree?
    My love of course is away
as Shakespeare once must have sighed.
    But this tree has such individuality.
It would hold my attention I feel
    almost any day of the year.

Fred Beake

Breakdown

Above Saddleworth Moor
grey snow-drenched hills
merge without definition
into pewter skies.

The motorway pulses constantly,
yet the moors retain their desolation
and silence is louder than engines.
Heartbeat louder than silence.

Isolation suffocates me.
Hills close in with pressing fear,
and the rusty mantle of my car
gives no protection.

Flimsy residual warmth from the journey
chokes and splutters
as fresh snow hurtles at the windows.
And gales buffet remaining inner stillness.

The small car clutches the road with despairing grip.
Lights dim as battery power drains.
Sobs rise, unbidden, unheard
and foolish fear adds stiffness to frozen limbs.

I think of the long dead children
buried in these moors
and pray that their souls were blessed
before God forsook this place.

Liz Poyser

Hope springs …

After the tight fold – a gentle unfurling,
after the darkness – a lengthening light,
after the bare branch – a tender greening,
after the empty nest – a hatching.

Now the eye perceives the land's relief
in the balm of a warm easing
and the heart finds hope in its belief
of a gradual sweet release.

After the climb – a looking ahead,
after the earth's tilt – a shift of key,
after the change – the moon brings in
a tide – of possibility.

                                    Susan Clark

No Need for Fine Feathers

A bargain it was
that bolt of cloth,
bought from a gypsy
at the door.

The old treadle whirred,
producing curtains, table
cloth, cushion covers and
Horror of Horrors,
a puffed sleeve dress for
my High School dance.
I wanted to die.

Decked in sky blue gingham
I fitted in at home, especially
In the kitchen.
Not so in the Assembly hall.
Standing, kin to a sore thumb,
among the taffetas and satins,
I wanted to hide.

Luckily the boy next door arrived
and claimed me as his partner.
Each other's port in a storm we
were, comfortable together.
I had almost relaxed

when Tom gasped 'Would you look at
her, I must have some of that.'
There stood Fay in layers of pink net,
looking to me like a spare loo roll doll.
I just wanted to run.

Until Tom uttered 'Just the thing for
keeping the blackbirds off the strawberries.'
Then he smiled and pulled me close and …
I wanted to be there.

Fiona McFadzean

Nursing Creature of the Deep

My infant son was dead before he breathed,
A fish forever in a sea of sand.
As lifeless as the ocean his stars seethed,
So beach him in a boat without a land.

A fish forever in a sea of sand,
He trod no shifting dunes, if dunes mean days.
So beach him in a boat without a land;
His wreck no more, since parent duty pays.

He trod no shifting dunes, if dunes mean days,
His hour-glass breathes in heaven, ours on earth;
His wreck no more since parent duty pays
Into a milky paradise of birth.

His hour-glass breathes in heaven, ours on earth;
As lifeless as the ocean his star's seethed
Into a milky paradise of birth.
My infant son was dead before he breathed.

Wendy Webb

Field ...

you are captured,
by your perimeter footpaths,
but also on film,
exposing your seasons, your timeless changes,
in a hundred clear images.

An April sun rises and light filters through
the thin line of trees skirting your ditches.
A Labrador pup bounds through wild grasses,
disturbs a lapwing. Bluebells nod their frustration.

Ripened wheat whispers in dizzying heat;
high summer seductively plays her old game
till the harvesters come, working you over:
raked, baled and netted, your proud golden crop.

October floodwater spills on to your plain.
A dog, padding through sodden drills,
sinks to his haunches,
face gritted against the jarring of old bones.

December dusk and you freeze.
Frost shimmers beneath a veined moon
hanging large and menacingly low.
Silence adds to its mystery.
Melancholy waits by the worm-riddled fence,
hunkers down with the dark.

Dorothy Nelson

Terra, terra

Strange to think that something
as transparently aquamarine and slicked
with turquoise as the Mediterranean
should be named, in part,
after the Latin for earth

but that was when this sea-cradle
was Rome's lifeblood, its trade-routes
stolen from Phoenicia, Sparta, Greece
and the Levant; and its imperial money-mould
swapped hands in the markets of Carthage,
Alexandria, Byzantium, Iberia and Gaul –
reason enough for this stretch of treachery
at the centre of things to be called
the middle of the earth – that red earth
they fired to amphora, and pan-tile:
Italy's *terra cotta*.

And yet, more certain, more contained,
this slippery sea than that *terra incognita*
where Visigoth and Hun – wolves
circling wolves – grew mean-eyed on envy
and waited patiently for erosions of will.

And not as indefinable, this sea, as that
where Iberia gave way to landless horizons
at the world's end, so named it *finisterre*.

Or as divisive as Caesar's Albion gamble,
that uncertain *terra firma* made secure
by history's cliché – *veni, vidi, vici* –
and lashings of olive and grape, oil and wine
shipped in for centurion and legionnaire
skulking in draughty camps
and getting maudlin-drunk
on memories of warmer shores,
lipped by lapis lazuli seas,
and earth the colour of spilt blood.

                              Roger Elkin

There You Have It

The sea is grey, the air is cold
the yellow sun is missing.

But every day that gorse is gold
the time is right for kissing.

                              Joy Howard

Lavash

Lavash is flour and water
and a little salt of friendship,
baked by the heat that remains
when the fire has raged and died,
and the endless patience of women.

The dough is rolled out flat
spread thinly on a cushion
and slapped on the wall of an oven
that is lined with a belly of clay
and dug in the mother earth.

In time it is peeled from the wall
and eaten soft and warm
or borne away with its twins
to be stored crisp and dry
against an hour of need.

Baptismal drops of water
will restore the bread to life
as companion to your meat
and to wayside bitter herbs
where you please.

Peter Sutton

Mouthing

A million words your mouth has uttered:
a mime triggered by a silent speech-chain,
stabbing muscles into movement;
contractions, nerve-lines galvanised,
all to mouth a million million words,
more than the stars in the Milky Way –
who knows? I have watched those lips.

A billion morphemes, grunts and fricatives
slamming teeth to tongue, gums to muscle,
throat sluiced and uvula vibrated,
scrapes and sweeps of all the effort
to mouth a billion billion articulations,
more than all the ants in a summer –
who knows? I have watched those lips.

A million times you called to others;
perfunctory squeaks and sighs.
Easy momentary release of wind and sound,
never to say that you love. Never.
I know. I have watched those lips.

Stephen Wade

The walk to the river

I'll show you the way, she says, *this afternoon.*

But I'll not go. Don't want be led. Would sooner
Get lost on my own (which, next day, I do).
The river, awkward as I am, seems to flow
Backwards, and the bridge has vanished.

The way I do find, I suspect, is as old as me.
It's cold. The sun tries hard. The water's clear.
But you are on the other side. What trim canoe
Will bring me over when it's time to come to you?

It scarcely matters. Whenever I step on board
I know you'll have the mooring ready,
The coffee freshly brewed, the whisky poured.

R. V. Bailey

Into Hiding

Hiding from me at bedtime, my daughter
sneezes and giggles from inside the wardrobe.
I wonder where she is, I act. Pretending
not to see her four small fingers clutching
the door but, fearing the dark far more
than she does me, she surrenders. I gasp
in mock surprise. Soon she will be sleeping.

In Germany once
whole families hid in cupboards
while friends pretended not to see.
But, so many years on, most would say
forget, forgive, let ancient horrors be.

Me? I am reminded tonight of the mother
who, on hearing footsteps on the stairs,
hurried her children into hiding; four hearts
thumping in a wardrobe.

Like mine, perhaps her daughter
would have giggled had she sneezed.
Sneezed and giggled, giggled and sneezed,
sneezed away four lives.

I smothered her so the others might survive.
It was Thursday, the ninth, in nineteen thirty
Nine. November, she says, I remember, thinking
even then how all her little movements
were as earthquakes when matched against
the stillnesses to come.

Brian Wake

The Junk and Disorderly and Shabitat Shops

were two places
you couldn't resist
and we didn't

checking the sizes
of red dresses
rummaging boxes
of something or other
while I pretended
not to be checking
a rather snazzy cardigan

a cardigan

which needless to say
was completely ignored
as over dinner
I started to whinge
about wasting our week
when there's so much to do
so much to see
then made the strategic error
of listing museums

she pounced

that's the same as those shops
using stuff again
the past is important
but recycling is now
so I'll do your museums
if you do something for me
you can start with those names
that made us laugh

it took me a month
to hand over an anagram
will this do

Dad helps John/buy a shirt/and donates skirt

She said be serious

Terry Quinn

Village of Dreams

If I were to build a village of dreams
Would I choose to echo Italianate villas,
A tribute to those hill-stepped pastel homes
Dressed with statues, fountains and flowers
But sited on a sublime Welsh river-mouth
Where light changes on the turn of the tide?
Paths meander to a bridged lake through
Magical rose-trees of so many shades
That it could be Asia that we've reached.
Rather than everyday drenching sunlight
There will be days of mysterious mist,
Soft times of sunshine, days of warmth
Driving rain, bitter winds brushing at edges
Of a sheltered pleat in the lovely coastline.
I would chose again that mysterious place
Where Welsh dragons fly and mermaids swim
There is a certain magic that brings me back.

Anne Steward

Fisherman's Cot

By a river, swiftly flowing,
under eaves in colours bright,
fairy lights in cosh curves glowing
smile upon our dreams tonight.

How romantic, how ecstatic,
conjuring such atmosphere,
having nothings mathematic
whispered softly in my ear.

Such a graceful compliment;
how my eager metabolics
long for further nourishment
from your tender hyperbolics.

Of all the images of feeling
that describe illumination,
cosh curves seem the least appealing
in my humble estimation.

Fitting more to engineering,
steelwork, mill or coal face sceneries,
fairy lights are too endearing
to be burdened with catenaries.

Thus it is, the form of hanging,
better things will follow later.
While we're lemon-cream-meringueing,
your trigonometricator,

when to dimness they incline
a simple trick will teach which gives
a certain way to make them shine –
by taking first derivatives.

Vince Smith

Contributor's note: The punch line at the end is a maths joke.
Take the first derivative of a cosh curve and you get a shine
curve.

Golden Eagle

Dear Golden Eagle,

You won't remember me, the little girl.
In fact I doubt if you even saw us
as we sat in the car without a sound
or a muscle moved as we looked at you.

I remember it well, how large you were
with that great hooked beak which could tear my flesh
as easily as it could crush a mouse,
and bear it away to your needy young.

On that post you looked so strong and regal
a foot from where, with bated breath, I gazed.
Each feather a testament to your name,
as you rested there with unblinking eyes.

Then all at once you left without a sound,
so we, like the fieldmice, could breathe once more.

Liz Mills

Miniature in Hermitage

A Fabergé bird,
skilfully crafted,
rests under crystal glass dome,
wings outspread,
intricately detailed feathers.
Small piercing eyes –
diamonds set in gold –
stare, unseeing.

Opulence and grandeur are her world.
Seasons known only by visitor attire –
the museum's temperature at preservation level.
She sees world's wealth, priceless treasures.

Nowhere to nest.
No need for preening.
She has sung her silent melody
six generations long.
And dreams of flight,
of softened wings,
of freedom,
the precious joy of catching a worm.

Liz Poyser

Having Just Met

we are two women, one orchid
on a running-late Northern train.
Strangers, we ginger this fragility
onto a window seat.
Too bright to be ignored, it casts
itself over our virgin conversation,
seems to shrug the breaking stops
and starts.

I didn't want it,
a gift from an old friend, she says.

A doleful eye peers from a length of stem.
I wonder if it will survive the disembark
in frigid Grange-over-Sands,
or lie abandoned in some salt marsh ditch
for sheep to find.
We try again with talk of travel cruise
ships she can name. Two women,
one orchid on a going-slow
Northern train.

Cynthia Kitchen

Wet Spring Bank Holiday, Dee Estuary

Most of the view you have to imagine
when grey presents its variations –
the opposite coast ghosting back.
Absent first are the field shapes,
a green collage of hills,
precise definition of copse and farm,
the massed browns of Holywell;
next, Moel-y-Parc retracts its long antenna.
Under a gauze of rain, the outlined hills –
curvilinear, cut-off, cauled –
disappear in the drowned distance.

From both the estuary's shores
this same shroud separating
coasts, cliffs, the sprinkling of estates
whose lights at night are fallen galaxies –
all dissolve in the vanishing trick.

The metallic Dee divides
yet magnetises shore to shore.
Staring across from each side, eyes
watch like wildlife in undergrowth;
or binocularised, strain to reduce the miles,
capture circles of someone else's space.
Dunlin, redshank, gull, in flight
link coast to coast invisibly,
alight on unseen sand-banks.

Always there's this yearning to connect –
the views are never sufficient,
yet every fade-out seems somehow a death.

Gladys Mary Coles

Cancellation

We regret to inform you
that you have been cancelled.
The exciting implementation
of the oblivion accounting system
renders you redundant.
Please return keys, pass and laptop
to HR this morning
and vacate the premises by noon.
We would like to take this opportunity
to thank you for your years of loyal service
during which your absence has averaged
0.23 days per year
and you have forsworn 3.17 days of each annual leave –
6.72 since the death of your husband.
You have been a successful parent.
Your children – adult, independent –
flourish with families of their own.
Since they live at a distance
which precludes frequent visits,
your responsibilities to them
are now negligible.
As for the choir, the reading group,
the allotment committee …
the friends you have within them
can fulfil your roles
and provide adequate support
for each other.
We therefore judge that a month is sufficient
to set your affairs in order
and you will, of course,
continue to be paid
until you then report
for cancellation.

Catherine Fitzsimons

Lost Souls and Angels

I was caressed by delicate white
butterfly wings and dust,
beautified warmth in remembrance
of lost souls and angels. Quilted

butterfly wings and dust
that summer after he'd left,
brought my father's memory alive.

Beautified warmth and remembrance,
flitting on flower fragrant buddleia
and my outstretched arms, holding a shimmer

of lost souls and angels,
fond fleeting moments carried
by the fragility of a butterfly's kiss.

                              Gill Hawkins

That time

Because sometimes it steals upon you
when you're looking in the window of a shop
or find you have ten minutes extra
to cool your heels before whatever it is
that might pizzazz the hour.
Strange to think it could be early morning –
that of a sudden, as the sounds of the first cars
wash across the walls, as the radio
bloats with worldly fecklessness,
you might be not there.

The day will maunder on,
dispensing the blitz of first love,
the leisurely burn of a million frustrations,
I-know-my-rights in bantam chorale,
the return of the prodigal or the oil-smeared cat.
Accord, boredom, defiance
will turn about their woozy poles.
A far part of the planet will cough up
a new species or relict of an age
fallen long since down the back of memory –
and you will no longer be in the thick
with a shake of the head or fancy-that goggle,
no longer start at a forgotten refund
or hear once again after months and months
that odd sort-of-squishing in the downpipe.
It always seems that twilight is fittest –
when sun and blue and heartbeat
can leave seemly and abreast
like three friends through the open doors
of a country pub in deep summer.
But it might be the other end.
You might enfold your everything
and let yourself noiselessly out
as brightness bests the municipal lamps
and the first pint rattles off the wagon.

Michael W. Thomas

Nightmares

All was well till her mind cracked.
I was a fine king: harsh, strong, quashing opponents;
rewarding loyalty, destroying dissension;
feasting and fighting, setting up spies …

And then her mind cracked. And through that crack
the nightmares forced their way back.
I had shut them away, cabin'd, cribb'd, confin'd them.
But they were back: oozing blood, knocking,
knocking at the door,
knocking at the door of my sometime soul.
Daggers, gouts of blood,
voices threatening my sleep, threatening my mind.
And the man no-one could see
standing there, or even sitting in my seat,
shaking his bloodied locks at me.

She was the strong one,
laughing at my fears, my visions,
my naked, new-born babes,
the knocking at the door, the blanket of the dark …
And now she sits there, day after day,
robed in majesty, unmoving, a stone effigy,
hands motionless in her lap.
Helpless, docile, like an obedient child.
Until the night.

I hear her rise and take the candle –
the light she cannot leave, for shadows must be fought.
She walks through hollowness, then pauses.
Places the light near. Then the rubbing begins.
Sometimes there is real water.
But usually it is only in her mind's eye.
And with the rubbing and the hand-wringing
she conjures up visions of her own:
the old man with so much blood in him.

No more 'A little water clears us of this deed',
but now 'Will these hands ne'er be clean?'
And like a fourth Weird Sister calling up apparitions
with her ceaseless hands, by the flickering light
she shapes and gives body to my nightmares too.

And so this bank and shoal of time
is all but flooded by the tides rising from the depths.

Elizabeth Horrocks

Ithaca, Odyssey In A Lunchtime

Unlike Odysseus
we didn't endure ten years
of storms, shipwrecks and angry gods
before we arrived here;
we just took a ferry.

Midday's heat finds us eating olives
and sipping Mythos beer
in an almost empty beach-front taverna.
Knowing it's not the time to intrude
wavelets barely lap the sand
as we sit, hands touching, eyes embracing,
recollecting our own journeys:
our totems of misfortune
and our exiles on islands of loneliness.

Unlike Odysseus
we didn't endure ten years
of storms, shipwrecks and angry gods
before we found our Ithaca;
we just took a lifetime.

Stephen Beattie

Lost Carnation of Andalucia

Seasoned by years, I meander
through Eastern markets,
a kaleidoscopic maze of silks and spices–

turmeric, saffron and sage.
Snakes uncoil and rise to a haunting
flute. I rewind to our cicada

nights, when your coal-black eyes flashed
and your red dress flicked with rhythm
to the wail and stamp of Flamenco.

Latin fire sparked to the clap of castanets,
flooding blood through youthful veins;
that night, our hunger danced to a crescendo.

Now, I lean on a crooked cane and capture
digital memories for grandchildren. Inside
I still ache for your flame.

Francesca Hunt

Bobbing for Snigs

The rain was merciless for days on end.
The strolling river became a swollen torrent.
The fields were sockwettingly sodden.

On Sunday the heavens had a day of rest.
Uncle Sammy, John and Dad decided this
was the time to go bobbing for snigs.

With sack, broom handle and washing line,
we squelched in wellies through muddy meadows
till we reached the bank of the turbulent Wyre.

An uprooted sapling sailed past on the flood
as my uncle assembled his broom handle rod
with a garish lure made from strands of wool.

The next passerby was a bloated dead sheep,
with stiff legs pointing to the angry sky
like an upside down Chippendale table.

Sammy cast his bait into the murky wild water
with dangling wool dancing to entice the eels
hunting earthworms dislodged by the spate.

As the float bobbed helplessly on the surface
a sinuous predator sank needle-like teeth
in our tempting bunch of woolly worms.

As Sammy heaved the startled fish hurtled
out of the water, hopelessly unable
to free itself from the Velcro like grip.

As soon as it hit the ground I pounced
and thrust it into the sack where Dad and John
disentangled it from the decoy worms.

Three hours later the sack bulged and wriggled
with the protests of thirty six seething serpents
who now wouldn't make it to the Sargasso Sea.
Instead all our neighbours had eels for their tea.

Mike Cracknell

Stranded

and anchored in a fretwork of foam
over sea-shimmering silver gilt sand
I'm bliss-basking like an old grey seal
beached and loving it

so till the seventh wave
lolls over me and nudges me back
to the sea   let your hands glide
over mounded flesh and soft pelt
while you plumb my fathomable eyes
and marvel at my stillness

believe me
I'm more graceful in water

Joy Howard

A Child's Illustrated Treasury

Once upon a time, a long, long time ago, in Manchester Art Gallery...

Miffy shuffles sideways
guided by an assistant who hisses irritably:
'Bend your knees. Bend your *knees.*'
But even then, the tips of her huge ears
brush against the door frame.

They have been doing this
for two weeks now
and though the galleries are cool
the heat today is breathless;
the children always shrill.

Inside, it is taking two of them to ease
the massive head upwards.
Outside, Mummy says firmly:
'Miffy's gone now.'
but the tiny girl inches forward …

Don't open the door.
Whatever you do,
don't open the door.

Carole Baldock

Melamine Dreams

B & Q label on melamine: 'I can be a shelf – but I dream of
being so much more!'

I am on the rack, tortured
by ordinariness. Make me your project –
you know you want to! I want to be
your labour of love. My virgin whiteness
is smooth and shiny. Pure.

Take me home, strapped to your white van.
Let me feel the caress of your power tool.
Thrill me with electric driver,
screw me with countersunk bit.

I could give you cupboard love
in the bathroom by mirrored vanity units.
My love-handled doors
shine in your world of gleaming chrome.

I need the support of your bracket.
It's Wednesday. You could get discount,
but please, don't discount my dreams.

Joyce Reed

The Poet's Companion

Must be in mint condition, not disposed
To hay-fever, headaches, hangovers, hysteria, these being
The Poet's prerogative.

Typing and shorthand desirable. Ability
To function on long walks and in fast trains an advantage.
Must be visible/invisible

At the drop of a dactyl. Should be either
A mobile dictionary, thesaurus and encyclopaedia,
Or have instant access to same.

Cordon bleu and accountancy skills essential,
Also cooking of figures and instant recall of names
Of once-met strangers.

Should keep a good address book. In public will lead
The laughter, applause, the unbearably moving silence.
Must sustain with grace

The role of Muse, with even more grace the existence
Of another eight or so, also camera's curious peeping
When the Poet is reading a particularly

Randy poem about her, or (worse) about someone else.
Ability to endure reproaches for forgetfulness, lack of interest,
Heart, is looked for,

Also instant invention of convincing excuses for what the Poet
Does not want to do, and long-term ability to remember
Precise detail of each.

Must be personable, not beautiful. The Poet
Is not expected to waste time supervising
The Companion. She will bear

Charming, enchanted children, all of them
Variations on the Poet theme, and
Impossibly gifted.

Must travel well, be fluent in the more aesthetic
European languages; must be a Finder
Of nasty scraps of paper

And the miscellany of junk the Poet loses
And needs *this minute, now.* Must be well-read,
Well-earthed, well able

To forget her childhood's grand trajectory,
And sustain with undiminished poise
That saddest dedication: *lastly my wife,*

Who did the typing.

U. A. Fanthorpe

A Desire To Express

from looking at paintings by Vincent Van Gogh
on his forthcoming 168th birthday

Perhaps I dwelt too long, not on the triumphs
of my dazzling stars, my golden blossom
freckling miles and miles, against chromatic laws,
the melancholy blue. Not on the utmost dignity
of living things or those who promise love
but look at me with eyes as wild as stones.

Perhaps deploring as I did, the hollowness
of praise. Perhaps I probed too eagerly
the indeterminate for signs of certainty,
extreme desire to express how love and friendship
are the interplay and harmony of yellow flowers
in a yellow vase, how repetition is the only form
of permanence that nature can achieve.

But on how streaming time flees from us
as the seasons turn from green sensations
into monochrome and test the task of the unbiased
eye to see much more than what exists, transpose
a glint of starlight into paint. Detach the meaning
of a bed and rustic chair from where to rest or sit
into a test of light on light, relationships

And shapes against a field of cypresses or grass
with butterflies, their just-perceptible distortions
made to analyse appearance and illusions just as real
as loneliness and anguish too impossible and history
too soon to be completely understood.

Brian Wake

The Persistence of Water

As it nears the brim, water does not know
that gravity's pull will soon rip it loose,
send it in jumbled bewilderment
cascading earthwards. It does not know
its strength and beauty or its ability
to break a fragment of light in its prism.
It neither knows nor cares if it carries life.
It hacks, gouges and burrows underground
leaving particles of calcite behind
to beautify places that few will see.
It does not know why it carves, scrapes, cajoles
the landscape in rapids or meanders
or why it measures time in stalactites.

John Mills

Dawn Departure

She leaves, running lightly down the steps
– The door closing silently behind her.
The lark in her sings, while the owl blinks
His bleary eyes, and opens a mouth wide enough
To catch the dawn and swallow it down.

Anne Sheppard

Catch a falling star

I am collecting memories like lucky pebbles in the pocket of a
                                                        winter coat.
Moments honeyed; warm as whispers.
A secret treasure chest amidst the debris.
I want to bring them back,
To hold them in cupped hands,
Breathe new life on them,
Feel them glow, revive and live again in heart and mind.
See again for the first time the night view across Victoria Harbour,
Listen to the symphony of the Super Trees in Singapore Bay,
Watch the sunset on Aldeburgh beach,
Swim with my dad in Suffolk tides.
I want to be waiting for Leonard to skip on stage to caress me with
                                                        his words.
I want to pose again for that photo with my children by my side,
Smiling in the sunshine.
I want to hug my poetry for the first and best time,
I want to turn the corner in the hospital to see my daughter with her
                                                        baby:
Shock of golden hair, warble of new-born cry, first touch of milky
                                                        skin.
I want to bathe after my operation, soapy water healing the hurt.
I want to hear the call of his love echoing through lost years.
I want to be 12 years old and dancing to Perry Como,
Believing that I could:
'Catch a falling star
Put it in my pocket
And never let it fade away'.

                    Jacqueline Woods

Land of Trees

I have come to a wilderness place,
land of brambles, boulders,
land of trees,
far from the lure of town,
far from home.

Time here is the measure of trees,
their vapour breath, the ways
they splay their branches, leaves
waiting for a wind,
a splash of sun,
and how they drink the rain
daylight long,
then let the darkness run
its waters on their skin
down to the roots. They moan
in their sleep; they dream
birdsong under leaves,
fires, nights of snow,
and years like ocean waves
that ebb and flow
as they draw ring upon ring
deep within.

Irene Thomas

The Shopping Year

January brings the sales –
cheap Christmas cards, new bathroom scales.

February peddles wine
and roses for your Valentine.

Then March – it can't be Easter yet!
And spring already? Don't forget

that April is the time to plan
for summer – strappy tops? fake tan?

bikinis? No, thanks, not today –
you'd never think that we're in May.

Not autumn fashions? It's too soon –
I mean, we're still in flaming June.

And who on earth goes out to buy
their back-to-school stuff in July?

It's August, but those retail bullies
are plying us with winter woollies.

And what's this? Tinsel in September?
Please ... let's keep Christmas in December.

October – it's a choice between
Bonfire Night and Halloween.

No wonder that November's bleak –
how come Black Friday lasts a week?

December – don't tell Santa's elves …
but hot cross buns have hit the shelves.

Karen Pailing

The Reading

French is over, netball's been called off.
Outside, air crackles with ominous storm;
white lightning fractures the darkness
of an early afternoon in summer,
when all the classroom lights are on.

Restless thirteen year old girls don't worry
Miss Cartwright. She knows how to captivate;
and confident we aren't yet too proud
to be read to, invites us to scribble
in our rough books, or just rest our heads

on our desks, while she reads to us –
from The Eve of St Agnes.
We are transported to Gothic worlds,
conjure lives that will never be lived,
hide from the storm in a realm of dreams.

Shelagh MacKinnon

Blanks

are what she gave me
over the counter in 'Fast Film'.

'We don't charge for these,' she said
as I gazed into dense-black sliding
through her fingers.

I imagine where your head might be
among those dangerous hills,
tossing back a head of poet's hair
on our journey of quotations.

Was it this blank that showed you
sloped against a larch
telling of high-minded things,

that rare walk without a photo
as my claim to fame?

This assistant cradles your ghost presence
in her hands
'Do you want to keep these prints?'

she'd never understand.

Cynthia Kitchen

Mother Care

'I'd like a pair of those rubber gloves,'
says my Mother (aged eighty-four),
and during the next ten minutes or so
says the same thing four times more.
The 'rubber gloves' are just napkins, which
are folded and stacked in a pile;
the waitress brings us a pot of tea,
with a false and indulgent smile.

This is the mother who taught me well,
to love literature and art,
who can't remember my children's names
but knows 'Adlestrop' by heart.
She used to be so intelligent,
I'm often heard to explain;
until a couple of months ago
there was nothing wrong with her brain.

In her day she'd been a magistrate:
highly respected, and clever.
Retirement had brought new challenges;
she was always busy. However,
we leave the café, our roles reversed;
me, with a child whom I love.
I denounce senility and then ...
wipe my eyes on a rubber glove.

Jayne Osborn

I'll always be

I'll always be the child
In that Liverpool Council house
Family elsewhere.

A grand day out was by bus
Through the bombed, besmirched, brick fields
of Anfield, Everton, Kirkdale,
To Greek Street, by the Bullring,
Where we'd walk hand-held, to London Road.

Coffee and cake in the cafe at TJ's,
Before browsing for fabrics, buttons and zips,
In the bazaars up to Islington,
For her to measure, cut and sew for her living.

On a High Day,
She'd buy pea-pods in brown bags
From the biddy by the Pier Head.
We'd shell and eat them like sweets
And watch the boats
Before getting the bus back.

She'd had nine kids,
In fourteen years,
On her own.
Grandfather at sea.
No Welfare State.

Hell is here, she'd say,
You don't need to wait
For the afterlife.

She was four feet ten
And I was lucky to have been loved
By this giant of a woman.

Phil McNulty

Buckle Shoe Dance

Witch, twitch, grimbleclitch,
Stir up the cauldron with a switch
Cleaved from an elm at dead of night,
Seared by the moon to bright bone white.

Call up your sisters, bid them prance
Skirts a-swirl to the buckle shoe dance,
Skinny knuckle fingers patterning the air,
Clatter crack spike nails twist and tear.

Heel toe scrunch on rustle dry leaves,
Banshee cackle as the snake dance weaves,
Cobwebs drift where shadows lie,
And clutch at a witch as she swishes by.

Witch, twitch, grimbleclitch,
Stir up the cauldron with a switch
Cleaved from an elm at dead of night,
Seared by the moon to bright, bone, white.

Shirley Tomlinson

Tango

Moving each day to set patterns,
watching light glimmer through windows
flicker on breakfast things, the cutlery
sings its clattering cadence,

and after, walking the streets
feeling a pattern of gold on my flesh.
The zing of it,
sting of it as the sun climbs higher.

Archway of days. The mist in my senses
persuades me to dance, forget brittling bones,
the small ache of sadness. Just swing with it
cling to it, keeping the music inside.

My hands are my mother's, stack dishes,
turn a tap on, water leaps with a passion
like blood through my veins. I am old, I am young,
with songs strung through my days.

Cornflowers and poppies bloom in the barley
gold light on grasses, blue tone of memories
moving to swingtime. Sun and moonlight
with tango tight rhythm, all the days dancing.

Doris Corti

The Four Seasons

Winters packed their cold round childhood.
We would watch from lamplit rooms. The snows
Had their bleak comforts, had stillness,
But their 'For Ever' lied.

As we grew Autumns warned us
Of harvests ahead. That glasshouse, school,
Would force our crop, because ripeness is all.
Golden, but fallen, that promise.

Late now, to lie in the sun
With a book or bottle – ah, dreams rather than visions!
Is pleasant. Summers' memories, imaginations
Warm us till we are done.

But where, where is Spring?
The looked for, the long predicted, the not yet here?
The flowering, the sunburst, where?
When comes our awakening?

Colin H. E. Wiltshire

Being There

On the morning-moist edge of Chase Woods
fallen conkers are protected in their
green sputnik cases, lying in a firebed
of wounded autumn leaves. Under the rising sun
the trees are black; to each side a painter
has daubed the canopy with diffused orange.
My dog is a steam train running against
a barrage of birdsong. I'm a margin of nostalgia
in some spent photograph.

The sloping rows of blackcurrants drop an arc
to the meadow, the gaps between shining
as warming ice, as dew and light live their
daily awakening. There is a reproduction of shadows
in this molten waving motion of vision.

On this church-chime Sunday, it doesn't
matter if we loved once; it doesn't matter
if we've never met; it doesn't matter if our
paths will never cross again. What matters
is that when I exhale this, you sense the air,

my breath the failing breeze you feel.
When I look to the far spire you too will see
across the fields with me, there on the book
in your hand, on every single wall you own,
in whatever direction you care to look.

It's the only important thing this ennobled moment:
Being there.

Ronnie Goodyer

Linguistics

I didn't know how to translate between
the languages of cherry and mesquite,
or how a starry yucca could comfort me
            when I had no lilac.
My grandmother's flowers were all I knew –
            daffodil, tulip, iris.
I learned how much earlier iris could turn to rose,
but without shade, without useful watering,
blooms would come early or never
            appear at all.
The sounds of birds were always robin,
            wood-thrush, wren.
Those surely were not the words I heard
            from dove and mockingbird.
The scent of Queen Anne's lace
            was blessedly the same,
but I still needed to learn dust-smell,
            wind-smell.
It was like trying to learn Spanish
and being confused by words from my
            forty-years-gone French classes.
We never even get our senses programmed
            before we change it all.

                    Amy Jo Schoonover

This is just to say …

Apologies all round

I have polished off
the last of the Easter egg
which you were probably
saving for a treat

Made of finest Belgian chocolate
voted *Tesco's* Best;
it had to be ordered online
because the shops had run out.

And remember the time you woke me at 1am
because of the Easter Bunny?
Was the cunningly concealed egg
in fact from yesteryear?

Forgive me,
you weren't there to ask.
But you worry so about sell by dates,
and after all, it is the 29th of July.

Carole Baldock

From the Shoes up

She worked herself inside me from the shoes up
from that point she became real
and I was no longer me.

The rest were just accoutrements:

Mrs Betterton's Restoration cheeks,
Hippolyta's Tudor bum roll, big hair,
the loud 70s pregnant chainsmoker,
and the fifties mum having her hair done,
Miss Framer, clutching her cardi as she tapped tremulously on the
                                                                door.

The mint-sucking gran with her feather boa,
the Scots one pouring yet another 'nice cup o tea.'
Cleopatra with an asp at her breast,
a gin-swigging lesbian murderer,
Chorus, emerging from the audience –

They were all inside me:
the play was the thing
and the audience could laugh or cry
until the shoes came off.

              Liz Mills

A Weeping Landscape

The earth was bleeding
– wept falling bricks.
Flames gushed to heaven,
erased the stars and moon.
Planes loomed black in a blood red night sky,
persistent in their mission of destruction.
Like wasps around a sticky picnic cake,
they kept coming.

Death was a daily occurrence.
Yet I – a child – was unconscious
of the fear that fettered adult minds.
One day I wandered
through a changed landscape;
valleys and mountains of bricks,
a cemetery of homes
where twinkling windows once welcomed,
families now dead or parted.

There was a quietness –
a strange deceptive peace.
The only movement came from smoke
that snaked through rubble,
surrounded the curly head of a doll
sprawled in debris.
I wondered where its owner was,
ran to my mother,
went underground as a siren's plaintive cry
wailed its warning.

Dylys Osborne

Tomorrow's Tide

We watch the water,
cold and slow in waveless menace,
ease the sunless sand.

Sky-grey, between black ripple
at rocks and groins,
part of this breathing thing.
Here and gone
and here, a touch of spittle
foams the mad unsmiling edge
of barnacled life.

We chill, as cracked light deserts,
in weak, last-gasp, decline,
from black cloud haze
of rain, beyond the west.

Humourless-tired,
we pack the rods,
head for tree-line
shelter, oil lamps glow.
Small fish, fried. Wood smoke.
Tobacco heat and beer.
Where we see to the end of things.
And drink to tomorrow's tide.

Phil McNulty

This is a piece of purely functional poetry. It was written at the request of Blaenau Gwent Council prior to a series of outdoor poetry workshops in Bryn Bach Park. 20.6.04. At the last minute they decided they needed a...

Risk Assessment

The whole enterprise is fraught with hazard
When you come to think about it. No parent
Would ever let their child participate
Knowing the full extent of the danger.
Huddled for an hour in a sweaty tent
With only a poet to take care of them?
They could be inappropriately touched,
Approached by some ungodly reprobate
Offering to show them skylarks in return
For a quick peep at their budding talent.
They might catch fire; rub two ideas together
And – *poof!* – spontaneous creativity!
Addiction is a possibility
And the susceptible may find themselves
Unable to resist the strong compulsion
To indulge repeatedly in the habit.
For, as the wise poet wrote on the packet,
This stuff can seriously affect the heart.

Ann Drysdale

Contributor's note: The quoted line is by Elma Mitchell in *This Poem* from *People Etcetera*.

The Seagull

The seagull cast his prehistoric eye
  upon the feast beneath,

Wheeled round and landed squarely
  on the bench's back,

His large pink feet with claws protruding,
  sharp and hooked,

He cocked his head, his eye dilating
  as he summed them up.

The woman flapped her hands,
  'go go, shoo shoo!'

The man beside her waved his hat,
  the prehistoric eye stared back.

The seagull jumped onto the seat,
  and lunged his head towards them,

He opened wide his yellow beak
  and uttered forth a warning.

Alarmed and worried by his stance
  they shuffled back along the bench,

Without a thought she threw a chip,
  the seagull seized it roughly.

'He knew you would' the man rebuked her,
  So in a fit of pique, she threw another.

The seagull with the prehistoric eye looked up
  as others flew in overhead,

The couple screamed and threw the lot,
  as the feathered army landed.

Anne Sheppard

River Exe mussels with chilli, tomato and parsley

The foreplay is with warm bread and olive oil:
you dripped,
I licked my lips like a cat.
Then the mussels arrive
with just-opened steam
and a light dandruff of parsley.
You drool slightly
before choosing, teasing
the dark, hard lips
to reveal a first soft pearl.
You suck its sweetness
leaving a light aftermath
of garlic.

The Exe has done its work well.

I cross my legs
as you pluck and prick
with your perfect poet's fingers,
slipping them between
teeth and tongue tip
dipping into the oil slick
finger-bowl –
in out, out in, dripping
frivolity, not necessity.

O lucky bowl.
O lucky tongue.

You will spoon the juice slowly
saying the spice is just right
the flavours lingering:
'Just hot enough.'
If only he knew.

We refuse dessert.

Dawn Bauling

Incident on Thassos

The earthquake hit the shore at noon
but made no impression
on our mountain path
between Panagia and Limenas.

We strolled in the sun
then sheltered in the shade of olive trees.
Dark purple stink lilies
spread the smell of death
while pink oleander buds burst,
seeking the summer light.

Through the soles of our sandals
we felt the stony track
and watched a tortoise lumber across it,
head peering from side to side
from under his shockproof shell.
Way down through the trees
we saw the turquoise sea
and golden sands of Skala Panagia.
Then we stared across to the solid stone
acropolis walls
bearing the weight of time.

In Limenas, for twenty-seven seconds
water sloshed in the harbour,
buildings trembled but stayed connected
to the shaking street beneath,
shop windows shimmered but none shattered.

Beneath the ruins of the temple
on the edge of the agora,
Dionysus stirred in his sleep.

Bill Lythgoe

Our Caff

Melamine tables and tubular chairs,
safe little cubicles under the stairs.
The tables were damp and the music was loud
but once you were there you were one of the crowd.
Straight after school, if we had any cash
and the weather was bad,
we would all make a dash.
Charlie and Michael and Margaret and me.
Two coffees, a milk shake and one mug of tea.

We go now on Saturdays, after the match,
to argue and talk about how we can catch
the teams who are much higher up
in League One. Of chances we missed
and how we should have won.
It's still just the same, all the warmth and the steam,
the smell of the coffee and how it would seem
to always be welcoming, always the same.
A haven awaiting the end of the game.

There are other cafés now, modern and swish,
where you can get latte and Danish or quiche.
Some even have tablecloths, napkins and such
but none of them seem to appeal half as much
as our favourite caff, and it's managed somehow
to stay just the same and we still go there now.
Charlie and Michael and Margaret and me.
Two coffees, a milk shake and one mug of tea.

Dennis Bryant

The Bottles

Each of the bottles is filled with water.
This is important to remember.
They may bear different names on the labels.
They may appear to be different colours.
But each of the bottles is filled with water.

They stand in a line on a stall
in the far corner of the market.

The first woman comes,
and buys one of the bottles.
She thinks the bottle contains wine.
She takes it home to drink with her husband.
They end the night tipsy with ecstasy, falling
into each other's arms.

The second woman comes,
and buys the second bottle.
She thinks the bottle contains perfume.
She takes it home and sprinkles it
on her arms and on her neck.
She smiles at the men who smile at her,
thinking they can smell the scent
that she cannot smell.

The third woman comes,
and buys the third bottle.
She thinks the bottle contains medicine.
She takes it home and gives a spoonful
to each of her sick children.
The next day their eyes are laughing
as they sing and play in the street.

The fourth woman comes,
and asks for water.
The stall-keeper shrugs and points at the labels.
The woman unscrews the largest bottle, the one
with the water dyed the most exotic colour,
the one with the highest price on the label.

'I'll take this one,' she says, and stands
where she is and drinks every drop.
The stall-keeper, brazen-faced, still asks for his money.
The woman bends down and picks up a stone.
'Here is a loaf of bread,' she says.

Dave Ward

For the Journey

He packed a shirt, coarse woollen socks,
shaving brush and pen; dark brandy,
pipe and a screw of opium.

Between his garments, he layered
sheets of clear water, damp green light,
purple shadows and snow-sharp mountains;
his broad northern vowels wrapped in brown paper.
He travelled south to unaccustomed sun.

From this scuffed, much-dented case, he would release
the music of lakes, hiss of polished ice;
lonely clouds, the water colour spill
of melt from those familiar hills.

Margaret Gleave

Tinker, Tailor?

Anonymous
in his dishcloth mac,
he waits for a day of fog
to take his balding head
and thickening waistline
to a crossroad.

Should he allow himself
to be swallowed alive
by a flirt of scarlet lipstick,
after dinner port in Green Shield glasses,
and an identity concealed
in the false bottom
of a shabby suitcase,

or should he opt
for sneakoscope eyes
glued to vodka shot spyholes,
the checkmating clatter of stiletto heels
across a bed-sit floor,
and a Russian alias cooked up
in the lift-shaft reek of cabbage soup?

Rejecting both, he relocates
to an obscure parish in the fens,
and plucks names at random
from two separate pages
of the telephone directory.
Three years on, they appear
against prize winning cacti
at the County Show.

                              Corinne Lawrence

Travel in Hope

I don't want to be a woman who crochets,
politely plays Bridge every Thursday,
or completes The Times crossword
every morning before ten.

I want to be an adventuress, when sudden longings
race with abandon around my mind
like impetuous gusts of wind across a lake
or whip fallen leaves into a sandstorm.

I don't want to join girls' nights out,
where women set their stall with slap and bling,
watch the Kardashians and read *50 Shades of Grey* –
sooner stand in a post office queue.

I want to see inspiration in everything,
use pain to ignite my passion,
seek fresh worlds through my imagination,
search for uniqueness in myself and others.

I don't want to discuss age.
I want a mind that never slows down,
is fuelled by fearsome curiosity and a sense of wonder;
and when I'm old and someone says *we can't live forever*
I'll say, *we'll see about that* …

Carol Blanche Featherstone

Situation Vacant

A vacancy has arisen
for an experienced poem,
well versed, articulate,
equally qualified in truth and beauty.

The successful applicant
will possess profound communication skills,
and be typed single spaced
on one side of the paper only.

It shall have a working knowledge
of iambic pentameter, and be willing to undertake
advanced courses in dactyl and trochee management.

Duties will consist of arranging
the best words in the best order,
whispering through stillness,
and making sense of the universe.
A little light alliteration may also be required.

Payment is modest,
but accommodation between hard covers
will be provided.

Fringe benefits include
editorial feedback, spell checks –
and guaranteed immortality
for the right candidate.

                    Alison Chisholm

INDEX OF POETS

Fiona McFadzean	42, 80
Shelagh MacKinnon	70, 115
Phil McNulty	118, 127
John Mills	22, 111
Liz Mills	93, 125
Dorothy Nelson	18, 83
Jayne Osborn	38, 117
Dylys Osborne	65, 126
Patricia M. Osborne	33, 64
Karen Pailing	59, 114
Peter Phillips	67
Peggy Poole	57
Liz Poyser	79, 94
Terry Quinn	16, 90
Denise Randall	37
Mike Rathbone	44
Joyce Reed	63, 107
Ceinwen Sanderson	41
Amy Jo Schoonover	26, 123
Anne Sheppard	111, 129
Vince Smith	40, 92
Anne Steward	91
Peter Sutton	36, 86
Irene Thomas	34,113
Michael W. Thomas	62, 98
Hilary Tinsley	15, 72
Shirley Tomlinson	54, 119
Stephen Wade	26, 87
Brian Wake	89, 110
Dave Ward	28, 134
Wendy Webb	82
Andy Williams	46
Colin H. E. Wiltshire	31, 121
Jacqueline Woods	48, 112
Neil Zoladkiewicz	14

ACKNOWLEDGEMENTS

R. V. Bailey *The Little Wood – A Scrappy Little Harvest, Indigo Dreams Publishing, 2016, The walk to the river – Credentials: New and Selected Poems, Oversteps Books 2012;* Dawn Bauling *River Exe mussels with chilli, tomato and parsley* and *Stick Gathering at Golitha Falls, Shippen, IDP 2013;* Lucinda Carey *Moon Rise Again – The Dawntreader, Faint Remains of Existence, IDP 2013;* Alison Chisholm *Situation Vacant – Mapping the Maze, Headland Publications 2004, When Did We Last? – Echoes in Cloud, Caleta Publishing 2019;* Malcolm Chisholm *The Crich Tram – Poet's England 21 Derbyshire, Headland Publications 1999;* Gladys Mary Coles *The Cuttings – Liverpool Folio, Duckworth 1984, Marigolds Grow Wild on Platforms, Cassell 1996, Wet Spring Bank Holiday, Dee Estuary – Poet's England 22 Wirral, Headland Publications 2002;* Doris Corti *Summer Rain – Kingfisher and Other Things, Scriptora, Tango – Avenue of Days, Scriptora;* Beryl Cross *Young Turner at Brentford – Forty Minutes Late at Pont L'Évêque;* Martin Domleo *First Memory – Lapwing Publications 2014;* U. A. Fanthorpe *Rising Damp – Standing To, Peterloo Poets, 1982, New and Collected Poems, Enitharmon Press, 2010, The poet's companion – Neck-Verse, Peterloo Poets 1992;* Yvonne M. Fee *Four O'Clock Fantasy – Eating Your Cake and Having It, Fat Chance Press 1997, Prima Magazine 1994, 101 Poems to Get You Through the Day (and Night), Harper Collins;* Margaret Gleave *Cardiosophy – A Year of Leaves, For the Journey – A Year of Leaves;* Ronnie Goodyer *Being There – Forest moor or less, IDP 2020; Let's Not Go Out On This Winter Day, Indigo Dreams Revisited, IDP 2010;* Gill Hawkins *The Loneliness of Snowmen – Writing Magazine 2018;* Elizabeth Horrocks *Bottom's Dream – Lighten Up On Line;* Joy Howard *Stranded – Running Before the Wind, Grey Hen Press 2013, Foraging, Arachne Press 2017;* Corinne Lawrence *Respect – For the Silent, IDP 2019;* Bill Lythgoe *Time On His Hands – Creative Writing Ink Website 2017;* Fiona McFadzean *Doon the Watter fur the Fair – Greenock Writers' Club 50th Anniversary Anthology 2016, No Need for Fine Feathers – Litereight Anthology, Scots* version – *Greenock Writers' Club 50th Anniversary Anthology 2016;* Phil McNulty *Tomorrow's Tide – Focus Magazine 2018;* Liz Mills *Golden Eagle – Writer's Cafe 2019;* Dorothy Nelson *Journey – Poems in the Waiting Room 2011, Field ... – Bluebells in Winter 2018;* Jayne Osborn *Mother Care – Biscuit Poetry Prize Winners Anthology 2001, Literary Review 2010, Forgetting Home, US Anthology 2013, Putting my Affairs in Order – Light;* Patricia M. Osborne *Sunrise Concertante – Sarasvati Magazine, IDP 2017, Taxus Baccata, Hedgehog Poetry Press 2020;* Peter Phillips *Forest Fox – Poetry London;* Peggy Poole *Lessons from an Orchard – Windfall, Kettleshill Press 1994;* Terry Quinn *from the walls of Chicago Library, The North 2018, The Junk and Disorderly and Shabitat Shops, Acumen 2011;* Mike Rathbone *No Day Returns – Marigolds Grow Wild on Platforms, Cassell 1996;* Joyce Reed *Melamine Dreams – Iron Book of New Humorous Verse, Iron Press, 2010;* Amy Jo Schoonover *Linguistics – Common Threads 2020, Song of Summer – The Blue Tree, Ohio Poetry Day 1991;* Vince Smith *Fisherman's Cot – BBC Radio Network Northwest;* Peter Sutton *Lavash – Poems of Armenian War and Peace;* Irene Thomas *Land of Trees – Creative Mind – Nature Anthology 5, Preeta Press 2020;* Hilary Tinsley *Not Forgetting Grandad – Smiths Knoll;* Shirley Tomlinson *Buckle Shoe Dance – Hubble Bubble, Wayland 2003;* Dave Ward *The Bottles – Can You Hear anthology , Oxfam/PanMacmillan 1992,What Will They Give You – The Big Book of Christmas, Macmillan 2005;* Jacqueline Woods *Broken – Writing Magazine 2020;* Wendy Webb *Nursing Creature of the Deep – Writing Magazine;* Colin H. E. Wiltshire *The Four Seasons – Acumen.* Many of the poems in this book have also won awards and prizes in a range of competitions in Britain and America.

Lightning Source UK Ltd.
Milton Keynes UK
UKHW010657160223
417122UK00019B/1797

9 781312 946514